ideals®

MOTHER'S DAY

D1612148

Vol. 50, No. 3

Publisher, Patricia A. Pingry
Associate Editor, Tim Hamling
Art Director, Patrick McRae
Contributing Editors, Lansing Christman, Deana Deck, Russ Flint, Pamela Kennedy, Heidi King, Nancy J. Skarmeas
Editorial Asst. Donna Sigalos Budjenska

ISBN 0-8249-1108-3

IDEALS—Vol. 50, No. 3 May MCMXCIII IDEALS (ISSN 0019-137X) is published eight times a year: February, March, May, June, August, September, November, December by IDEALS PUBLISHING CORPORATION, P.O. Box 148000, Nashville, TN. 37214. Second-class postage paid at Nashville, Tennessee, and additional mailing offices. Copyright © MCMXCIII by IDEALS PUBLISHING CORPORATION. POSTMASTER: Send address changes to Ideals, Post Office Box 148000, Nashville, Tenn. 37214-8000. All rights reserved. Title IDEALS registered U.S. Patent Office.

SINGLE ISSUE—$4.95
ONE-YEAR SUBSCRIPTION—eight consecutive issues as published—$19.95
TWO-YEAR SUBSCRIPTION—sixteen consecutive issues as published—$35.95
Outside U.S.A., add $6.00 per subscription year for postage and handling.

ACKNOWLEDGMENTS

THE BUMPS AND BRUISES DOCTOR by Edgar A. Guest from *A HEAP O'LIVING*, copyright ©1916 by The Reilly and Lee Co. Used by permission of the author's estate. APRIL from *AUNT HATTIE'S PLACE* by Edna Jaques, copyright © in Canada by Thomas Allen & Son Limited; Our Sincere Thanks to the following authors whom we were unable to contact: Marie Hunter Dawson for TRANSIENT; Florence Ellison for LET'S PRETEND; Sudie Stuart Hager for MATERNAL SONG; Mildred Jarrell for MOTHER'S KITCHEN; Bertha Kleinman for IF I COULD GIVE YOU A PERFECT DAY; Myrtie Fisher Seaverns for GOD'S GARDEN; Grace V. Watkins for IF YOU HAVE TAUGHT A CHILD; and Eleanor Halbrook Zimmerman for GRANDMOTHER'S KITCHEN.

Four-color separations by Rayson Films, Inc., Waukesha, Wisconsin.

Printing by The Banta Company, Menasha, Wisconsin.

The paper used in this publication meets the minimum requirements of American National Standard for Information Sciences—Permanence of Paper for Printed Library Materials, ANSI Z39.48-1984.

Unsolicited manuscripts will not be returned without a self-addressed stamped envelope.

Inside Covers
Frances Hook

Front Cover
Al Riccio

IDEALS   MOTHER'S DAY 1993

April

Edna Jaques

The wind is whispering April,
    And the woods are all aflame.
Today a robin sang for me;
    From southern lands he came.
He brought the springtime with his song
    And practiced it the whole day long.

The sun is whispering April,
    And the buds are swelling green.
The little creek is running wild
    Its foolish banks between.
The pussy willow's silver fur
    Is making vain the heart of her.

And we have tidied all the yard,
    Raked up the tangled grass;
The little pool that father made
    Shines like a looking glass,
Reflecting sky and clouds and trees,
    The neighbors' clothesline if you please.

The wind is whispering April,
    And all my heart is knowing
There will be clover in the fields
    And new grass growing,
Daffodils on a sturdy stem
    And golden bees to talk to them.

SPRINGTIME STREAM
Toccoa, Georgia
Fred Sieb Photography

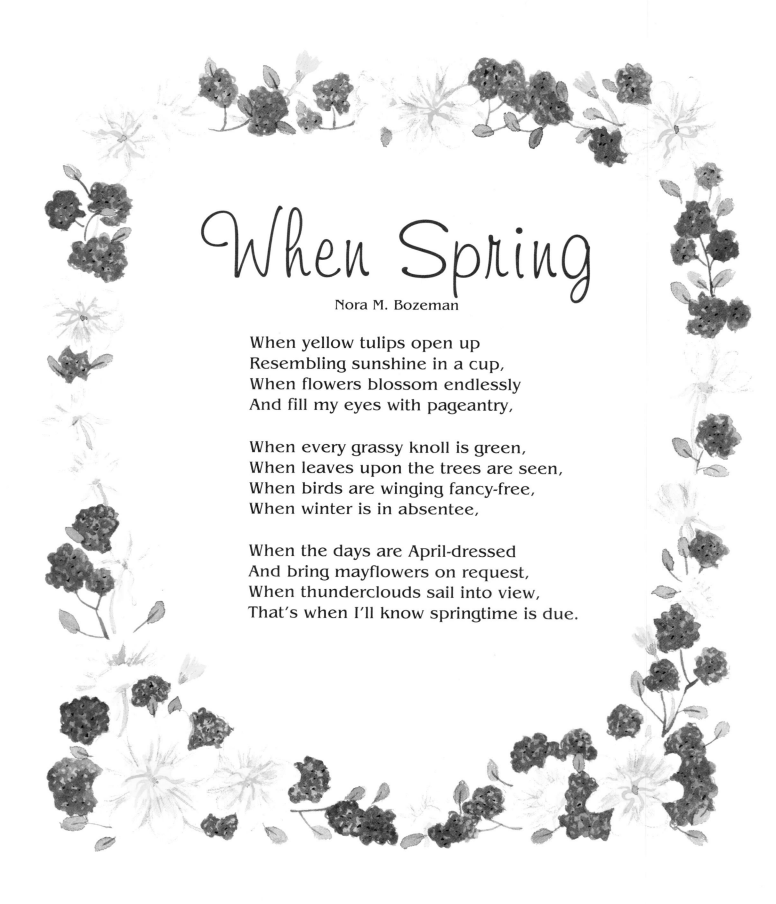

When Spring

Nora M. Bozeman

When yellow tulips open up
Resembling sunshine in a cup,
When flowers blossom endlessly
And fill my eyes with pageantry,

When every grassy knoll is green,
When leaves upon the trees are seen,
When birds are winging fancy-free,
When winter is in absentee,

When the days are April-dressed
And bring mayflowers on request,
When thunderclouds sail into view,
That's when I'll know springtime is due.

Photo Opposite
WHITE DUNES PRIMROSE AND PURPLE SAND VERBENA
Anza-Borrego State Park, California
Bob Clemenz Photography

Spring's Arrival

Marilyn Tullys

What would we call a blue-gold hour
When limbs drip silver from a shower
And fertile earth drinks in her gift
As blades push up and soft winds drift
To chorus songs across the land?
This time when music swells as leaves expand,
Lavishing new life on the land?

What would we name a tender day
In drizzly April, flowery May,
When sighing hearts with hope delight,
When all the world seems to invite
Skipping, rolling, frolicking?
What else could it be but spring?

Lady Springtime

Marianna Jo Arolin

Lady Springtime proudly wears
Her fresh pastels and lace

And dances through the meadows
With aromatic grace.

Then with her grandest fashions,
She dresses eager trees

And welcomes songbirds home
To sing their melodies.

8

Photo Opposite
BLOSSOMING CRABAPPLE AND BIRDHOUSE
North Conway, New Hampshire
Fred Sieb Photography

Heartthrob of Spring

Ruby Phillipy

Beneath a cherry blossom canopy,
My questing heart finds blessings
    rich and free
As sunbeams dance and peek through leaves
    In pleasant hide and seek
And leave a gentle kiss upon my cheek,
As though by chance.

I know delight in Nature at her best;
Her matchless beauty is made manifest
In winsome ways, as flowers make debut
    To charm us all,
Responding to the season's protocol
On spring-swept days.

When birdsong harmonies enchant the air,
The zephyrs waft ambrosial scent most rare,
And whispering of fragile wings
    Makes softest lullaby;
Then heartthrob of the quickened earth
    comes nigh,
For it is spring.

The Wind

Robert Louis Stevenson

I saw you toss the kites on high
And blow the birds about the sky;
And all around I heard you pass
Like ladies' skirts across the grass.
    O wind, a-blowing all day long,
    O wind, that sings so loud a song!

I saw the different things you did,
But always you yourself you hid.
I felt you push, I heard you call,
I could not see yourself at all.
    O wind, a-blowing all day long,
    O wind, that sings so loud a song!

O you that are so strong and cold,
O blower, are you young or old?
Are you a beast of field and tree,
Or just a stronger child than me?
    O wind, a-blowing all day long,
    O wind, that sings so loud a song!

Photo Opposite
SPRINGTIME FLIGHT
San Francisco, California
Superstock, Inc.

What Is the Grass?

from *Song of Myself* by Walt Whitman

A child said *What is the grass?*
fetching it to me with full hands;
How could I answer the child?
I do not know what it is any more than he.

I guess it must be the flag of my disposition,
out of hopeful green stuff woven.
Or I guess it is the handkerchief of the Lord,
a scented gift and remembrancer
designedly dropt,
Bearing the owner's name
someway in the corners,
that we may see and remark,
and say *Whose?*

Or I guess the grass is itself a child,
the produced babe of the vegetation.

GARDENS

Margaret E. Sangster

The wide, fair gardens, the rich, lush gardens,
    Which no man planted and no man tills;
Their strong seeds drifted; their brave bloom lifted,
    Near and far over vales and hills.
Sip the bees from their cups of sweetness,
    Poises above them the wild, free wing,
And night and morn from their doors are borne
    The dreams of the tunes that blithe hearts sing.

The waving gardens, the fragrant gardens,
    That toss in the sun by the broad highway;
Growing together, gorse and heather,
    Aster and goldenrod all the day.
Poppies dark with the wine of slumber,
    Daisies bright with the look of dawn,
The gentian blue, and the long year through,
    The flowers that carry the seasons on.

The dear old gardens, the pleasant gardens,
    Where mother used to potter about,
Tying and pulling, and sparingly culling,
    And watching each bud as its flower laughed out.
Hollyhocks here, and the prince's feather,
    Larkspur and primrose, and lilies white,
Sweet were the dear old-fashioned gardens
    Where we kissed Mother and said "Good-night."

FROM MY
G·A·R·D·E·N
JOURNAL

Deana Deck

Miniature Roses

Roses have always been associated with Mother's Day, but for me, they evoke even stronger associations with grandmothers—mine and those of my childhood friends. While I was growing up, our grandmothers' gardens, arbors, and picket fences overflowed with roses. They always placed crystal vases or silver pitchers brimming with roses in a place of honor at the center of the Sunday dinner table. Our grandmothers always pinned roses to their jackets when we went to town or to church and took along gift bouquets of roses in Mason jars when we went visiting. Our mothers were always busy cooking, cleaning, and chasing after our little brothers and sisters; but our grandmothers could usually be found on warm spring mornings lovingly caring for a rose garden of fragrant blooms. To me, the scent of roses is the scent of grandmothers.

Roses, however, require a lot of work; and the time invariably comes when gardening becomes more of a chore than a pleasure. Fortunately, the miniature rose is standing by to come to the rescue. Instead of requiring the gardener to haul bags of peat moss, fertilizer, hoses, rakes, shovels, and pruning shears around the garden, miniature roses can be tended with a pair of sewing scissors and a watering can.

For those who find rose culture an essential ingredient for happiness—and the numbers are legion—the miniature rose offers an opportunity to retain the joys of a rose garden without the physical labor. The tiny plants and their enchanting blooms, described by such appropriate names as "Cinderella," "Baby Gold Star," "Pixie Rose," "Sweet Fairy," and "Tinker Bell," are exact replicas of the floribunda and hybrid tea roses of the garden; and, like garden roses, they are available in a variety of forms and colors. There are cascading, climbing, and trailing varieties in addition to the tiny shrub forms and miniature tree roses.

Unlike the garden rose, the miniature rose will not lie dormant all winter and leave you bereft of blooms for several months. If kept in full sun in a south-facing window or under fluorescent grow lights, a miniature rose will remain in vigorous bloom all winter, with just a short time-out for resting.

This rest period can be provided by either placing the plants in a refrigerator for about eight weeks during the hottest part of the summer or by setting them outdoors for a couple of months in fall. By using both methods and rotating your plants, you can keep some in bloom at all times. The rotation method is also useful if you want to feature a bloom in a part of the house that does not receive enough sunlight to keep it healthy. Just use two plants and let them take turns in the sun.

For those who cannot provide the amount of direct sun that miniature roses need for indoor culture, the plants can be raised outdoors. Grow them on patios or balconies, in tubs, window boxes, or strawberry jars, or in the garden in easy-to-care-for beds. Cascading varieties are lovely in raised beds; they can either climb a short trellis or cascade down the sides of the planter.

When grown outdoors, miniature roses will gradually go dormant in late fall, but they can be mulched, covered, and cared for more easily than full-sized roses. In many cases, their containers will be small enough to facilitate moving them into a garage or basement for overwintering in extremely cold climates.

Before putting your miniature roses to bed for the winter or sending indoor plants into a rest period, prune the plants back to about three inches above the soil. When returning the miniature roses to the light, the pot can be placed under a plastic bag for several days to provide extra warmth and moisture. To avoid fungal diseases, remove the bag when the first leaf buds appear.

Although I always picture roses growing in the heat of a June summer day, in reality, all roses prefer cool temperatures. Consequently, it is easy to maintain an indoor garden of miniature roses because the temperature and humidity levels most suited to human health and comfort—seventy-two degrees and fifty percent humidity—are those which best suit the rose. If you are fortunate enough to have a bright, glassed-in sun porch that cools to sixty or sixty-five degrees at night, you will experience excellent results from your plants.

Keep the atmosphere around your miniature roses moist by placing the containers on gravel or sand in trays. Keep water in the bottom of the tray, but not enough to reach the bottom of the pot. Plastic pots are better than clay ones because it is easier to keep the miniature roses evenly moist. If the atmosphere becomes too hot and dry, spider mites can infest the plants. Fortunately, the pest can be controlled with a commercial aerosol spray.

Anytime of the year is perfect for adding miniature roses to your gardens. They are available at all garden centers and can be mail ordered from most reputable growers. Since they are winter hardy, miniature roses can be shipped year round. As the scent of their fragrant blooms fills the air, remember your grandmother and her passion for beautiful flowers.

Deana Deck lives in Nashville, Tennessee where her garden column is a regular feature in The Tennessean.

HELP ME IN THE GARDEN

Craig Sathoff

Please help me in the garden,
Little grandson, small and fine.
There are rows to hoe and seeds to sow,
And the weather is divine.

There's a vision of lettuce growing
To serve with vinegar and cream.
There are small potatoes and new peas
To add luster to our dream.

Please come and help me garden,
Granddaughter, sweet and fair.
There are onions that need setting,
And there is lilac in the air.

A vision of harvest's bounty,
Of pumpkins, beans, and squash,
Of carrots to store in crocks of sand
And canning jars to wash.

Please share with me this special time
When there is gardening to do,
And we'll enjoy the grand rewards
That last the whole year through.

GRANDMOTHER'S KITCHEN

Eleanor Halbrook Zimmerman

With its potted plants and its curtains white,
Grandmother's kitchen is our delight.
There are cakes with spice, and apple pies,
And little brown cookies with raisin eyes;

Dishes to lick and jam to spread
On the brown and crusty homemade bread;
And to crown it all, the smiling face
Of Grandmother, queen of this happy place!

She doesn't mind when we romp and play
And get hungry a dozen times a day.
She never complains about the noise,
But says, "Never mind, young girls and boys!"

Though storms may come and wind may shout,
Warmth and laughter will shut them out;
And the day, when it's gone, seems scarce begun
Because Grandmother's kitchen is so much fun!

Mother's Kitchen

Mildred L. Jarrell

I love my mother's kitchen;
It's always bright and gay,
With flowers on the windowsill
To brighten up the day.

The kettle gaily singing,
The shining kitchen floor,
The smell of spice and homemade bread
When you open up the door.

I love my mother's kitchen,
For the family gathers there;
The laughter and the joy we share
Are way beyond compare.

The other rooms in our old house
Hold comfort, peace, and rest;
But my mother's homey kitchen
Is the room we all love best.

Photo Opposite
COUNTRY KITCHEN TABLE
Jessie Walker Associates

Ideals' Family Recipes

Favorite recipes from the *Ideals'* family of readers

Editor's note: If you would like us to consider your favorite recipe, please send a typed copy of the recipe along with your name and address to: *Ideals* Magazine, P.O. Box 140300, Nashville, TN 37214 ATTN: Recipes. We will pay $10 for each recipe used. Recipes cannot be returned.

CINNAMON RAISIN COFFEE CAKE

Preheat oven to 325°. Grease an 8 x 11-inch pan and set aside. In a mixing bowl, mix together ¾ cup of brown sugar, ½ cup of sugar, and 1 tablespoon of cinnamon and set aside. In a second bowl, sift together 2 cups of flour, 1 teaspoon of baking soda, and 1 teaspoon of baking powder. In a third bowl, combine 1 cup of buttermilk and 1 teaspoon of vanilla. In a fourth mixing bowl, cream together 1 cup of sugar and ½ cup of margarine and add 2 eggs.

Add ¼ of flour mixture to creamed mixture; then add ⅓ of buttermilk mixture. Continue adding the flour mixture and the buttermilk mixture alternately to the creamed mixture, but begin and end with flour mixture.

Spread half of the cake mixture in the greased pan and sprinkle with half of the brown sugar topping. Spread the remaining cake batter over the topping and top with the rest of the brown sugar topping. Sprinkle top with raisins. Bake in 325° oven for 40 minutes. Remove from oven and let cool slightly.

Evelyn Goblet
North Aurora, Illinois

HONEY-COCONUT COFFEE CAKE

Preheat oven to 350°. Grease a 1½-quart casserole and set aside. In a large mixing bowl, combine ½ cup of flour, 1 package of instant yeast, 2 tablespoons of sugar, 1 teaspoon of grated lemon rind, and ¼ teaspoon of salt. In a saucepan, heat ⅓ cup of milk, ¼ cup of water, and 2 tablespoons of butter. Add liquid to the flour mixture and then add 1 egg. Blend batter at low speed until moistened, then beat for several minutes at medium speed. By hand, gradually stir in 1 cup of flour to make stiff batter. Cover and let rise in a warm place until batter doubles (about 30 minutes).

While batter rises, in a small saucepan combine ⅔ cup of flaked coconut, ¼ cup of sugar, ¼ cup of butter, 3 tablespoons of honey, 1 tablespoon of milk, 1 tablespoon of chopped toasted almonds, and ⅛ teaspoon of vanilla. Simmer topping over medium heat for 1 minute and allow to cool.

Stir down batter. Spread it in a greased 1½-quart casserole. Cover batter and let rise in a warm place until it doubles (about 30 minutes). Spoon topping onto batter and spread to within one inch of edge.

Bake in 350° oven for 30 to 35 minutes (until edges are golden brown).

Anne Schaefer
Miami, Florida

APRICOT COFFEE CAKE

Preheat oven to 425°. Grease an 8-inch round cake pan and set aside. In a large mixing bowl, combine ½ cup of brown sugar, ¼ cup of walnuts, 2 tablespoons of margarine, and 2 tablespoons of grated orange rind. Place, cut side down, one 16oz. can of apricot halves, drained, in the greased cake pan. Sprinkle with the brown sugar mixture. Arrange one package of 10 refrigerator biscuits over the brown sugar mixture.

Bake in 425° oven for 8 to 12 minutes. Remove from oven and let stand for a few minutes. Invert the pan on wax paper and allow coffee cake to cool slightly before lifting pan.

Heidi Hedman
Nashville, Tennessee

Only One Mother

Garnett Ann Schultz

Only one Mother, a lifetime through,
Though so many other things come by two.
The rainbows, the starlight, the beautiful things,
Each new tomorrow, another one brings.

Plenty of roses and sunsets and such,
Green grass and blue skies that still mean so much.
The sunshine of summer is waiting for you,
Another bright springtime when winter is through.

But only one Mother, God meant it this way,
That she should be special and dearer each day.
He took part of all in this world bright and real
And made them a part of the Mother ideal.

Do cherish this treasure, so precious and rare,
For she has a heart and is willing to share.
God's greatest creation, more dear than all others;
All else comes in dozens, but only one Mother.

NATURE'S TREASURE, Ralph Crowell, Photographer.

Country CHRONICLE
—— Lansing Christman ——

There is intense love in the sound of the word "Mother." Edgar Allan Poe wrote long ago that "the angels, whispering to one another, can find, among their burning terms of love, none so devotional as that of 'Mother.'"

My own mother has been gone for nearly half a century, but I feel in my heart that she is forever near. I can see her tending and nurturing her plants and shrubs, her flowers and ferns.

I can see her cooking and baking in her gingham apron. I remember the tantalizing aroma of pies—apple, custard, coconut, and pumpkin. She made cakes and pans of cookies—sugar cookies, molasses and oatmeal cookies, and gingersnaps. We were always privileged to have a cookie or two when they were still warm. The rest went into the cookie jar, but we were familiar with its location in the pantry. I remember the huge loaves of hot, homemade bread. Nothing seemed better than a slice of that freshly made

TULIP GARDEN, Gene Ahrens, Photographer.

bread covered with melted butter.

I can see my mother mending by lamplight in the evening. I remember with adoring admiration her sparkling brown eyes and her pure white hair. She often hummed some of the enduring hymns that we continue to hear in churches today. I often recall how she comforted and consoled me in my young years.

She left me a wonderful heritage. She taught me the identity and beauty of wildflowers, from spring's trailing arbutus and hepatica, to summer's Queen Anne's Lace and the evening primrose, to autumn's festival of goldenrod and asters. She taught me to identify birds and their lovely songs and to love the hills and woodland streams.

I continue to live in hills, although not in those of my boyhood; and I continue to hold in my heart a love for the hills I knew for sixty years. Now I am in these newer hills, hills I have known for the past twenty-three years. I love them too, and their flowers and birds and purling streams.

On this Mother's Day, I am especially grateful for the precious legacy my mother left me—an enduring love for the outdoor world that continues to be an essential part of my life.

The author of two published books, Lansing Christman has been contributing to Ideals *for almost twenty years. Mr. Christman has also been published in several American, foreign, and braille anthologies. He lives in rural South Carolina.*

Woodland Ballerinas

Brenda West

SHOWY LADY'S SLIPPER, Apostle Island National Lakeshore, Wisconsin, Michael Shedlock, Photographer.

Years ago, my mother used to walk my two younger brothers and me to school. Since we lived in a remote area surrounded by dense woods, we felt secure when Mom accompanied us. I remember enjoying those impromptu tours, especially in springtime, because I knew school would soon end; but Mom unknowingly instilled a different kind of joy which I did not fully appreciate until much later.

During our daily walks, we watched impatiently for new stirrings of life as the frozen earth yawned slowly awake. Mom would pause to look for wildflowers waiting to burst forth from a blanket of melting snow and brown twigs.

"Kids," Mom announced one morning, "looks like spring is here. There are the first snowdrops."

Three pairs of eyes gazed skeptically in the direction of her pointing finger. Sure enough, like a symbol of hope, a clump of tiny, white bell shapes contrasted sharply with the black, leaf-strewn earth. Within a few days, the rocky slopes

34

were dotted with the prolific flowers. As the season progressed, Mom exulted daily at the spectacular panorama that nature so generously unveiled—tiny violets nestled along the old barbed wire fence; dazzling white Mayflowers, coquettish under their umbrella-like leaves; showy lady's slippers; and jaunty jack-in-the-pulpits. All made their long-awaited debut.

The world looked fresh and inviting on those long-ago mornings as the sun cast warmth and light along our path. Birds twittering from lofty nests seemed to pay homage to their Creator. Our paradise was alive with sound and beauty. Even at that young age, I felt a sense of awe, as if I were being allowed a special, undeserved gift—one of peace and serenity that would not always grace the future.

As the years passed with new experiences, I gradually forgot the delicate snowdrops, velvet violets, flowery lady's slippers, and the satin-black jack-in-the-pulpits until a few years ago. My daughter and I found two blooming lady's slippers spaced a few yards apart on a steep hillside. We were hiking, unaware of the beauty lying at our feet, and literally stumbled upon them.

How to describe the unexpected delight? Serendipity, some might reply. The sight of that splash of color partially hidden in the undergrowth brought an odd mixture of reverence and elation—the rare feeling of having discovered a treasure.

Pinkish white in color, the rounded blossoms dangled gracefully from tall, leafy stems. The flowers actually resembled a soft-soled shoe adorned with intricate laces—designed by nature for a miniature dancer.

"Woodland ballerinas," my daughter, Traci, exclaimed.

"A poetic description," I agreed.

At that moment, I was without my camera. Regrettably, by the time we had a chance to retrace our steps a few days later, the flowers had vanished.

The next spring arrived sooner than usual, with lush vegetation setting in before mid-May. The opportunity to search for lady's slippers eluded us. This May, however, we were deter-

mined. On Mother's Day, we found them! Several plants had sprung up on an adjacent hillside in various stages of growth. One was in full bloom, two were midway, and a few others remained tightly budded. They were the purple variety and slightly different in appearance from the pinkish white species. This vista, however, was still no less exciting than the first.

Oblivious to the dangers of lecherous ticks, angry bees, and prickly briers, I snapped plenty of photographs. When I emerged from the photo session, my hair stood on end, crushed twigs and leaves clung to my clothes, and my shoes were mud-encrusted; but the disadvantage of lying face down to get an angle on the lady's slippers was worth the effort.

Our hills are abundant with treasure, the kind that bears no price tag but brings satisfaction to the seeker. Wildflowers are one of the jewels and a privilege to behold. They are like old, dear friends—we're always happy to see them.

If
You Have Taught
a Child

Grace V. Watkins

If you have taught a little child
To love a hilltop where the wild
Blue columbine is heart's delight;

If you have shown him stars at night
And helped him feel the soundless grace,
The magnitude of time and space;

If you have led him up the stair
Of holy fellowship and prayer
And heard the chimes of heaven ring,
Then you have done a wondrous thing.

God's Garden

Myrtie Fisher Seaverns

When the wise God planted His garden,
Scattering the seeds from above,
The choicest seed in His packet
Was the flower of Mother-love.

Carefully watched o'er and tended,
Nurtured by sunshine and shower,
Ever growing sturdy and stronger,
It blooms—a beautiful flower.

A flower so sweet and entrancing,
Dazzling and shining and white,
A love that guards us and guides us
Through life—our beacon light.

A love that steadies our footsteps,
That stretches a helpful hand,
That comforts our sorrows and heartaches,
That always will understand.

Mother-love, God's gift to His children,
With heavenly fragrance fraught;
The brightest flower in God's garden,
His truest forget-me-not.

Readers' Reflections

Editor's Note:
Readers are invited to submit unpublished, original poetry for possible publication in future issues of *Ideals*. Please send copies only; manuscripts will not be returned. Writers receive $10 for each published submission. Send material to "Readers' Reflections," Ideals Publishing Corporation, P.O. Box 140300, Nashville, TN 37214-0300.

Mother's Flowers

Every day was Mother's Day
    When I was just a child.
Time at home when we would play
    Was joyous, never wild.

Mother made us dresses;
    Mother made us fudge;
Mother combed our tresses;
    She never let us judge.

Mother planted flowers;
    She tended them with care;
She knelt by them for hours;
    I think she said a prayer.

Her flowers were inspiring,
    For life was sometimes hard;
She weeded, never tiring,
    In those beds inside our yard.

Blossoms bright as rainbows
    Responded to her touch;
Her loving, caring hands chose
    To pinch, pull, break, and such.

Each flower's name was known;
    She made sure we understood
That the tiny seeds she'd planted
    Would grow and be so good.

I can see them now in memory,
    In both summer and in fall;
But Mother's flowers in springtime
    Were the very best of all.

Hannah Belle Baranich
Clarington, Ohio

Yellow Gold

The prettiest flowers I ever got
Came not from a florist's bouquet,
But from the hands of a little tot
On a mild summer's day.
They were only weeds from a pasture nearby,
Held clutched in a tiny palm.
Straggled and wilted and drooped they were
From the long and weary trip home.
But when I saw the shining face beaming up at me,
So eager to please as he said, "Mommy, here!"
They became more than weeds to me.
The yellow petals seemed turned to gold
As they glowed in the bright, shining sun.
And of all the flowers I've gotten since then,
I wouldn't trade a one for the beautiful weeds
I received that day, picked by my baby for me.
They're eternally wrapped and sealed with love,
Preserved in my memory.

Peggy Putnam
Hattiesburg, Mississippi

My Children Brought Me Roses

My children brought me roses,
Love gathered in a vase,
A glimpse of heaven surely,
Of glory and of grace.

My children brought me roses,
Their fragrance rich and sweet;
Within the heart of every rose,
My heart with God did meet.

My children brought me roses,
So beautiful, so fair.
It seemed my heart would overflow
To have a gift so rare.

These roses from their garden,
Raised with such love and care,
Each colored part a rainbow,
Each petal seemed a prayer.

Dorothy Heist Falk
Encinitas, California

41

My Mother's Coat

Susan E. DiVenti

The author and her mother, Luise Rathell.

There is something I have that is very special to me. It is soft and warm and heavy. It is the color of blushing pink roses and has round brown buttons that have a crisscross pattern like the tops of peanut butter cookies. The inside is a silky satin as red as rubies. It is many years old, yet is like new. It is my mother's coat, an engagement gift from my father to my mother over thirty-five years ago.

I recall how my mother always wore her coat to church on cold winter Sundays. I liked to snuggle against the velvetlike cashmere that smelled as clean and sweet as she. Sometimes, when the cold was too much for me, she would open her coat, enfold me in its warmth, and hold me close like a mother bird taking her baby under her wing. Peeking out from inside my warm cocoon, I would listen to the majestic notes sounding from the organ pipes. The voices of the congregation swelled in triumphant praise, but I could only hear my mother's sweet voice echoing inside as if she were singing only for me.

I remember using the coat when I would do my best pretending. With a crown of plastic flowers in my hair and my majorette's baton as my royal scepter, I would drape the coat over my shoulders and become Queen of the World, beloved by all. I would move in a regal gait throughout the house as the hem of my velvet cloak dusted the floor. My dolls and stuffed animals, the loyal subjects of my kingdom, would bow and curtsy as I passed them on the way to my golden castle.

I would imagine I was the winner of a beauty pageant. The train of my mantle flowed obediently behind me as I strolled in slow motion down the lighted stage. I waved and blew sweet kisses of victory to the cheering audience. The lilting sounds of the orchestra carried me along as the delicate scent of my floral trophy wafted around me. Then, I would suddenly become a movie star draped in my pink fur. As I stepped out of my limo, cameras would light up my face and my adoring fans would reach out to touch me.

Many nights I used the coat as my mystical rose petal against the cold. I could have had an extra blanket or a fluffy quilt, but those ordinary things just wouldn't do. At bedtime, I would ask my mother to cover me with my special comforter so that I'd be sure to stay toasty all night. Each time I asked, she would slip downstairs to the closet to happily fulfill my request. I could hear the door open and the screech of the metal hanger as she removed the coat. The door would close with a thud, and I would hear her soft footsteps on the stairs. I sank deeper into my covers and rubbed my cold little toes together in anticipation of the press of the heavy coat against my blankets. Carefully tucking me in to seal all the precious warmth of my body, she kissed me good-night and laughed softly to herself at the earnestness of my nightly petition. I drifted off to sleep knowing that I was protected from yet another winter night's cold by the magic of my mother's coat.

As I grew older and became more involved with school activities and new friends, I forgot about the coat and all the things it meant to me. It hung in the darkness of the closet; my mother never even wore it anymore. She had new coats to wear.

One day, I happened to be at my mother's house when she was cleaning out the closet. As she separated the redeemables from the beyond-help items, my eye caught a glimpse of something very familiar to me—my mother's old coat! My heart leapt at the sight of my long-lost friend. A flood of memories washed over me as I removed it from the hanger and wrapped it around me.

The old pink coat looked a bit tattered, to say the least. There were a few small holes in the cashmere, the lining was torn, and there were holes in the pockets. The buttons were dull and hung limply from their proper spaces. The hem was falling; all the threads dangled from the edge. This once-beautiful coat was now a shadow of its former self—a testament to what the passing years and an imaginative little girl can do.

I asked my mother if I could have it, tattered hem, torn lining, and all. She smiled at me and nodded, knowing all too well the thoughts that were going through my mind.

After a careful inspection of the coat's sad condition, I felt a slight sense of guilt at the injustice it had suffered at my hand. I vowed I would bring this precious relic back to life.

I took the coat to one of the best tailors in the city. I ordered a new satin lining and new pockets. The buttons were tightened and polished, and the tiny holes in the cashmere were repaired. The hem was sewn back into place; and, as a final touch, the coat was dry-cleaned to perfection. It took about three weeks for the work to be done.

Finally, the shop called, and I made the long trip downtown. I couldn't believe my eyes when they lifted the crinkly plastic wrapper and showed me the finished product. The work they had done was incredible. It was as if I were looking at a brand new coat, as new and as beautiful as the day my father bestowed it on his future bride.

I was so excited that I drove all the way to my mother's house to let her see the miracle that had taken place. In a wistful gesture for old times' sake, I offered to give the coat back to her; but she graciously said I deserved it after the loving effort I had put into its restoration. I kissed my mother's soft cheek and whispered a most grateful thank-you in her ear.

I wore my old friend on the long drive home. It felt wonderful—like a warm hug from my mother.

Let's Pretend

Florence G. Ellison

A tiny girl stole up to me
And asked me with an earnest plea
To come with her where sorrows end
Within the land of Let's Pretend.

44

She whispered, "You can play with me
Here in my home beside the tree."
But I only saw a boundary spaced
Where chairs and table had been placed.

She drew a stool up close to mine,
And in a voice so shy and fine,
She asked me if I'd stop for tea
And told me of her children three.

Some joys we miss by growing up!
For age has drained life's fullest cup,
And we find it hard to comprehend
The mysteries of Let's Pretend.

Mother's Voice

Marilyn Tullys

In my heart are messages
  which often I replay,
Treasured guidance wisely stored
  to guide me on life's way.
Words which parted wrong from right
  stay with me from my youth,
Words which taught a preference
  for kindness and for truth,

Counsel and encouragement
  for purpose that's fulfilled,
Soft echoes of phrases meant
  to undergird and build.

In my heart are messages
  which urge for Godly choice.
Within the caring lines inside,
  I hear my mother's voice.

Photo Opposite.
CARNATIONS, DAISIES, AND LILIES FOR MOTHER
Lefever/Grushow
Grant Heilman Photography

BITS & PIECES

Every man, for the sake of the great blessed Mother in Heaven, and for the love of his own little mother on earth, should handle all womankind gently, and hold them in all honor.

Alfred, Lord Tennyson

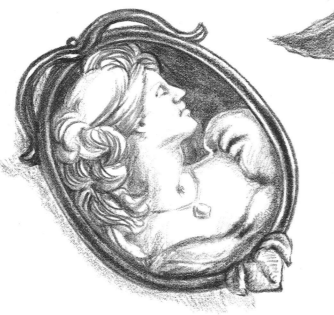

A mother's love is indeed the golden link that binds youth to age; and he is still but a child, however time may have furrowed his cheek or silvered his brow, who can yet recall, with a softened heart, the fond devotion or the gentle chidings of the best friend that God ever gave us.

Christian Nestell Bovee

Stories first heard at a mother's knee are never wholly forgotten—a little spring that never quite dries up in our journey through scorching years.

Giovanni Ruffini

I attribute my success in life to the moral, intellectual, and physical education which I received from my mother.

George Washington

Children, look in those eyes, listen to that dear voice, notice the feeling of even a single touch that is bestowed upon you by that gentle hand! Make much of it while yet you have that most precious of all good gifts, a loving mother. Read the unfathomable love of those eyes, the kind anxiety of that tone and look, however slight your pain. In after life, you may have friends, fond, dear friends, but never will you have again the inexpressible love and gentleness lavished upon you, which none but a mother bestows.

Thomas Babington Macaulay

Mighty is the force of motherhood! It transforms all things by its vital heat; it turns timidity into fierce courage, and dreadless defiance into tremulous submission; it turns thoughtlessness into foresight, and yet stills all anxiety into calm content; it makes selfishness become self-denial and gives even to hard vanity the glance of admiring love.

George Eliot

The seasons come
And the seasons go
And many the changes
      they bring,
But in the warmth
Of a mother's heart,
It is forever spring.

Barbara Burrow

49

Dear Lord! Kind Lord!

James Whitcomb Riley

Dear Lord! Kind Lord!
Gracious Lord! I pray
Thou wilt look on all I love
Tenderly today!

Weed their hearts of weariness;
Scatter every care
Down a wake of angel-wings
Winnowing the air.

And with all the needy,
O divide, I pray,
This vast treasure of content
That is mine today.

50

Photo Opposite
VICTORIAN SUN PORCH
Jessie Walker Associates

THROUGH MY WINDOW
Pamela Kennedy

Mother's Day Greetings

The racks are full of Mother's Day cards once more. Browsing through them, I find verses penned in bold calligraphy and dainty script, some with softly faded photographs and others with eye-catching graphics. There are so many choices; one could find just about any type of card for any type of mother. There are few cards, however, that will ever be as treasured as those children write in their own trembling hands in the years when they have learned to communicate through the written word but are still innocent enough to be totally honest about how they feel. I know because I have a collection of these cards garnered from the childhoods of my three children. Whenever I feel a bit down about my mothering, I bring the cards out and read them once again.

Probably the first Mother's Day card every modern-day mother receives is the one Sunday school and preschool teachers create each year. I have received variations on this card from each of my children. The card sports a hand print, or sometimes two, on a plain construction paper background. (I am still in awe of any teacher who allows a classroom of youngsters to run around with paint-covered hands.) Inside the folded paper is a copy of the following poem:

Sometimes you get discouraged
Because I am so small
And always leave my fingerprints
On furniture and wall.
But every day I'm growing up
And soon I'll be so tall
That all those little fingerprints
Will be hard to recall.
So here's a final hand print
So someday you can say,
"This is how your fingers looked
For Mother's Day in May."

I have no idea who wrote this little verse, but I know for sure that her kids were young. The reason I know is that fingerprints don't go away; they just move higher up the wall and eventually may even be found on the ceilings! The verse is a nice sentiment and something a first-time mother should receive at least once in her life.

After graduating from the hand print and mimeographed poem stage, the time comes for the best Mother's Day cards—the time when the children actually compose their own verses. In kindergarten and first grade, the mere fact that spelling is not refined makes for some interesting greetings. My son once gave me a card addressed to "the beast Mom in the hole world!" My daughter had a problem with writing letters backward and turned her *p's* around to wish me a "Very Haggy Mother's Day!" I would like to attribute their original greetings to mere immaturity and not to some Freudian slip.

During second and third grade, my children began to try their hands at poetry, and the verses they created on Mother's Day are the ones I read when I need to take myself a little less seriously. My son's third grade teacher compiled a leaflet of poetry containing an entry from each child in the class to his or her mother. The poems all followed the same pattern: the word Mother was followed by two adjectives, then a phrase or two describing something they admired about her, then closed with a synonym for Mother. I read through about twenty of these little gems and smiled at how tender and sweet they were. Then I

came to my son's. My nine-year-old realist had penned:

Mother
Loving, Caring
Helps me with my homework,
On a scale of 1-10, I give you a 7,
Mom.

I was not sure if that was a compliment or a complaint, but I expect he felt I had some room for improvement!

My daughter, Anne, prefers rhyming verse and came up with the following for her Mother's Day offering:

My Mother is very, very neat.
She is the person you'd like to meet.
She knows what love means.
She's always pretty clean.
There's nothing quite like a mother.
Not a sister or father or even a brother.

Anne is obviously not given to flowery words, nor is she prone to exaggeration—at least not in the case of my virtues! But there are certainly worse things to be remembered for than cleanliness.

My children are now a bit older and more sophisticated, and they have abdicated the role of greeting card writer to professionals. They thoughtfully choose sentiments properly aligned on bond paper and written in the smooth meter of the accomplished poet, but I still cherish the broadly traced script painstakingly scrawled on notebook paper. In the poetry of my children's cards, I find my affirmation as a mother. These are the people who live with me day in and day out, who know all my failings and still rate me as neat, clean, and a perfectly acceptable seven!

Pamela Kennedy is a freelance writer of short stories, articles, essays, and children's books. Married to a naval officer and mother of three children, she has made her home on both U. S. coasts and in Hawaii and currently resides in Washington D.C. She draws her material from her own experiences and memories, adding bits of her imagination to create a story or mood.

NINETEENTH CENTURY AMERICAN SAMPLER

American Samplers

Heidi King

Whenever I see examples of early American samplers in needlecraft books or museum collections, I picture a young girl sitting restlessly on the edge of her chair and trying diligently to imitate the intricate embroidery stitches made by her mother for use as

a pattern. I recall how impatient I became when my mother tried to teach me, and I can't help but wonder if the young girl had as much trouble suppressing her squirms and disregarding her daydreams as I did. I also wonder if ripping out less-than-perfect stitches agitated her as it did me—almost to the point that I would have been quite happy to misplace my embroidery and my mother as well.

Unlike the compendiums of stitches made two and three centuries ago, today's samplers are embroidered mostly for display and decoration. Early samplers, however, were "how-to" books on which stitches were practiced and recorded on a long, narrow piece of fabric that could be kept neatly rolled up in a sewing basket. Whenever a special stitch was needed to embellish clothing or mend household linens, this convenient reference could be easily consulted for the appropriate handwork. These pieces were not considered to be embroidery projects but rather a catalog of an adult woman's needlework vocabulary.

The origin of American samplers dates back to sixteenth-century England. Samplers were quite fashionable and an essential activity in the English courts since an excess of needlework was one of the more obvious ways to display wealth. By the seventeenth century, samplers had reached America and evolved into square and rectangular shapes that proved to be more manageable for young fingers. For this reason, handwork became a means for young girls to demonstrate their artistic skills instead of the precise stitches used by older women. Flowers, birds, poetic verses, and other decorative designs appeared. Borders also

became commonplace and are credited with transforming samplers from works of reference to display pieces.

Samplers were also standard teaching tools. Throughout most of the 1700s, a mother taught her daughters needlework at home; but toward the end of the century, girls were sent to private schools to learn the art. Teachers would draw a design for the school sampler, and under close supervision, the students would stitch the design. This type of schoolroom discipline produced carefully worked stitches and introduced the students to design and presentation. For many girls, education ended at these schools. Equipped with a basic knowledge of sewing, young girls were considered to be more useful at home where they could mark linens and clothing.

Also at the end of the seventeenth century, sampler stitchers began to sign and include genealogical information on their work, an addition that textile experts believe originated in the United States. Many needleworkers stitched their family's history—birthdays, dates of marriages, and the deaths of loved ones. Such samplers were on-going projects; important dates were added many years after the work was begun. Interestingly, when a young girl had grown into a young woman, she often removed the last two numbers of her birth date to conceal her age. Genealogists have found these samplers to be nearly as useful as a family Bible in tracing family trees.

Fancywork samplers composed of freehand embroidery in crewel and silk yarns continued to be favored in the eighteenth century; but practical samplers with the revived cross-stitch increased in popularity in the nineteenth century. The most recognizable of these is the "marking sampler," a pattern of numerals and letters sewn onto a piece of linen. This type of sewing enabled the young girl to practice her stitches and learn

NINETEENTH CENTURY AMERICAN SAMPLER

her numbers and rudimentary reading skills.

During the Civil War, sampler work virtually disappeared; but recently it has witnessed a revival due to its elevated status as an authentic traditional avocation. It has also regained popularity because twentieth-century samplers have become stylized with specific embroidery stitches that eliminate any guesswork on the needleworker's part. Stitchers who once found little time to allot to such a time-consuming hobby are now striving to keep an American tradition alive.

Heidi King contributes regularly to Ideals *and still becomes impatient with less-than-perfect stitches.*

A SLICE OF LIFE

Edgar A. Guest

The Bumps and Bruises Doctor

I'm the bumps and bruises doctor;
   I'm the expert that they seek
When their rough and tumble playing
   Leaves a scar on leg or cheek.

I'm the rapid, certain curer
   For the wounds of every fall;
I'm the pain eradicator;
   I can always heal them all.

56

Bumps on little people's foreheads
    I can quickly smooth away;
I take splinters out of fingers
    Without very much delay.
Little sorrows I can banish
    With the magic of my touch;
I can fix a bruise that's dreadful
    So it isn't hurting much.

I'm the bumps and bruises doctor,
    And I answer every call,
And my fee is very simple,
    Just a kiss and that is all.

And I'm sitting here and wishing
    In the years that are to be,
When they face life's real troubles
    That they'll bring them all to me.

Edgar A. Guest began his illustrious career in 1895 at the age of fourteen when his work first appeared in the Detroit Free Press. *His column was syndicated in over 300 newspapers, and he became known as "The Poet of the People."*

57

My Mother's Love

Joy Belle Burgess

Through the endless years of time,
Her love will always be
A citadel of quiet strength,
A pool of deep tranquility.

A fount of wisdom in the day,
A shining star in heaven's night,
The lambent flame of mother love
That guides my stumbling feet aright.

A place of refuge for the heart
When the skies have turned to gray;
A loving smile and warm embrace,
A prayerful thought to light my way.

A love that always stays the same
And forever blesses me;
As timeless as eternity,
My mother's love will always be.

FLOWERING RHODODENDRONS
Harkness Memorial State Park, Connecticut
William Johnson
Johnson's Photography

COLLECTOR'S CORNER

Tim Hamling

TEDDY BEAR COLLECTION, Ralph Luedtke, Photographer.

Teddy Bears

A teddy bear is a child's best friend and a mother's best helper—a dependable companion to accompany children everywhere and a watchful guardian to protect them. Their plumply stuffed bodies may be worn by years of hugging and handling, but their years of being lovingly cherished soon become years of careful preservation by avid collectors.

Who made the first teddy bear is difficult to determine, but its popularity can be traced to

Clifford Berryman's 1902 political cartoon that depicts President Theodore Roosevelt's refusal to shoot a tiny bear cub while hunting in Mississippi. The cartoon, which appeared in publications throughout the nation and became a valuable publicity item for the president, inspired a shop owner named Morris Michtom to make a small stuffed bear, ingeniously labeled "Teddy's Bear" after the president, and display it in his window. When the bear sold immediately and its replacements did the same, Michtom took his design to an American toy maker who began mass-producing the toy in 1903.

Morris Michtom would seemingly have the claim as the creator of the teddy bear, but a German firm named Steiff, founded in the 1880s by Margarete Steiff, also claims to have begun its production at the time. Steiff began experimenting with felt and soon produced a small toy elephant that she used as a pincushion. Steiff's friends were so enchanted by her design that they encouraged her to make others for their use; and in the following years, she designed several new animals—a monkey, donkey, horse, pig, and camel. When one of Steiff's nephews joined the firm, he encouraged her to make a toy bear with movable joints. Steiff initially disliked the idea; but when a toy buyer showed great interest in the toy bear in 1903, Steiff began mass-producing the teddy bear.

The earliest Steiff bears are often called "rod bears" because their head and limbs were attached to the body by a metal rod skeleton. They had very long arms, shoe-button eyes, a hard body, and a sealing wax nose. Steiff's trademark identification for its bears was a button in the ear. These buttons help distinguish Steiff bears from other manufacturers and aid in dating the bear. The earliest bears had a pewter button embossed by an elephant, clearly a tribute to Margarete Steiff's first creation.

Later Steiff bears contain cardboard joints to replace the rod skeleton. Their arms are shorter and curved to imitate paws. The wax noses have been replaced by stitched cotton floss, and the hard stuffing has been replaced by a softer mixture of kapok and excelsior. The bears made during this period, 1904-1905, have blank pewter buttons in their ears; those made in later years, 1905-1948, have glass eyes and a pewter button embossed with the Steiff name.

During Steiff's days of mass production, many American companies were also producing teddy bears, but they were less meticulous in identifying their bears. The Ideal Toy Corporation produced a great number of bears but gave them no identifying mark. In general, Ideal's bears had thinner bodies and more triangular heads than the Steiff models. Many of the bears had five floss claws embroidered on their paws. Two other American manufacturers, Aetna and Bruin Manufacturing Company, were also distributing bears, but they labeled theirs—Aetna with a stamp on the right foot and Bruin with a woven ribbon label.

The enormous number of teddy bears made in the last ninety years makes it essential to be well-informed before beginning a collection. Collectors should first consider a bear's condition. Obviously, teddy bears in mint condition are the most valuable. Check for thinning in the animal's mohair fur and for damage to the felt pads used to construct the paws. The more wear that is present, the lower the bear's value.

A teddy bear's monetary value also depends on its rarity. Light brown and cream colored bears are the most abundant. Rarer colors, such as cinnamon, white, and dark brown, are more valuable; and black and red bears are the most rare. Size also affects a bear's value. If condition, color, and other factors are all equal, larger bears are usually more valuable.

Teddy bears made by Steiff are generally the most desirable to collectors. Sales of these bears often generate record prices; one sold for an astonishing $86,350 in 1989. One noted collector suggests that pre-1915 Steiff bears be valued between $100 and $125 per inch of height.

Although many factors determine a teddy bear's monetary worth, simple memories determine its sentimental value. Teddy bears with slightly torn ears, a missing eye, and faded fur will be avoided by serious collectors; but these bears will have no problem finding a home with the children they accompanied and comforted through so many childhood adventures.

FOR THE CHILDREN

ARTWORK BY RUSS FLINT

When Mother Reads Aloud

Author Unknown

When Mother reads aloud, the past
     Seems real as every day;
I hear the tramp of armies vast,
I see the spears and lances cast,
     I join the trilling fray;
Brave knights and ladies fair and proud
I meet when Mother reads aloud.

When Mother reads aloud, far lands
     Seem very near and true;
I cross the desert's gleaming sands,
Or hunt the jungle's prowling bands,
     Or sail the ocean blue.
Far heights, whose peaks cold mists shroud,
I scale when Mother reads aloud.

When Mother reads aloud, I long
     For noble deeds to do.
To help the right, redress the wrong;
It seems so easy to be strong,
     So simple to be true.
Oh, thick and fast the visions crowd
My eyes when Mother reads aloud.

CHILD AND MOTHER

Eugene Field

O Mother-My-Love, if you'll give me your hand,
    And go where I ask you to wander,
I will lead you away to a beautiful land,
    The Dreamland that's waiting out yonder.
We'll walk in a sweet posie garden out there
    Where moonlight and starlight are streaming
And the flowers and the birds are filling the air
    With the fragrance and music of dreaming.

There'll be no little tired-out boy to undress,
    No questions or cares to perplex you;

There'll be no little bruises or bumps to caress,
　　Nor patching of stockings to vex you.
For I'll rock you away on a silver-dew stream
　　And sing you asleep when you're weary,
And no one shall know of our beautiful dream
　　But you and your own little dearie.

And when I am tired, I'll nestle my head
　　In the bosom that's soothed me so often,
And the wide-awake stars shall sing in my stead
　　A song which our dreaming shall soften.
So, Mother-My-Love, let me take your dear hand,
　　And away through the starlight we'll wander,
Away through the mist to the beautiful land,
　　The Dreamland that's waiting out yonder!

TRAVELER'S *Diary*

Tim Hamling

HOME OF THE OLD WOMAN WHO LIVED IN A SHOE. Photo courtesy of the Gingerbread Castle.

The Gingerbread Castle

What child would not want to travel to a magical land of make-believe where the fantastic dreams of his imagination come to life? A castle with walls made of gingerbread, a sugar-frosted roof, peppermint stick towers, icing turrets, and sugar-glazed windows seems like a creation of the wildest imagination, but such a treasure exists in the tiny town of Hamburg, New Jersey. The Gingerbread Castle brings childhood dreams to life for both the young and the young-at-heart.

Visitors to the Gingerbread Castle are greeted by young guides dressed appropriately as Hansel and Gretel. These expertly trained school children lead guests on a magical tour through the land of Make-Believe. Prince Charming astride his prancing steed greets the guests first as he protects the magical kingdom from fierce dragons. Perched high on a wall above the Prince is Humpty-Dumpty. As evidenced by the wide grin on his face and the absence of cracks in his shell, he has been magically restored by the spirits of the land of Make-Believe. At the turn in the path leading to the castle is a gigantic shoe surrounded by a colorful picket fence—obviously the home of "the old woman who lived in a shoe." She must have built the fence to keep track of her many children.

66

Once inside the castle, Hansel and Gretel lead their guests to the cellar where the wicked witch has placed spells on many well-known characters from favorite fairy tales. Before the witch can add to her collection, however, visitors are led to safety up a candy-coated staircase. Upstairs, each room of the castle brings a memorable scene to life. Dressed in her beautiful gown, Cinderella and her handsome young prince look as elegant as a king and queen. Little Bo Peep looks forlorn as she searches high and low for her sheep. Maybe someone will volunteer to help her look for them.

In another room, Little Red Riding Hood carries a basket of goodies to her grandmother, but first she must pass the wicked wolf lurking around the corner. The giant spider that frightened Miss Muffet away hangs from an immense web suspended high in the castle's turret, but it does not seem to bother Snow White and her seven dwarfs, who look as happy as the castle's wide-eyed visitors.

The hundreds of thousands of visitors who have enjoyed the treasures of the Gingerbread Castle owe their gratitude to its founder, F. H. Bennett. As a young boy, Bennett listened with amazement to the magical fairy tales his mother read to him. He never forgot these tales as he grew older, and he dreamed of turning the land of make-believe into a land that all children could visit and enjoy.

Bennett's dream persisted. In 1928, when he attended a stage performance of *Hansel and Gretel*, the spectacular stage settings by world-renowned set designer Joseph Urban inspired Bennett to construct a gingerbread castle to house the fairy tale characters he vividly remembered from his childhood. Bennett solicited Urban's assistance, and in 1930 he opened the Gingerbread Castle to the public.

The only construction of its kind in the United States and one of only two in the world, the Gingerbread Castle is a magical fairyland where childhood dreams come to life. Its many characters are based primarily upon the folk tales of the Brothers Grimm, but favorite figures from

THE GINGERBREAD CASTLE
Photo courtesy of the Gingerbread Castle.

the stories of Mother Goose and other fairy tales are also included.

By 1978, time and weather had greatly diminished the physical charm of the castle; it fell into disrepair until 1988, when Brian Hamilton and Joseph DiFiglia purchased the castle to restore it to its original splendor. The spirit that had originally inspired F. H. Bennett continued in Hamilton and DiFiglia as they worked to bring back the magical charm that had enraptured so many children and adults.

Today, the Gingerbread Castle amazes young children, who see their favorite stories come to life, and refreshes the memories of adults, who remember with nostalgia the tales they heard in their youth. "A monument to imagination, storytelling, and children," the Gingerbread Castle is truly a place where dreams come true.

Nancy Skarmeas

MCRAE

Margaret Wise Brown

As a child, Margaret Wise Brown spent long, blissful days playing in the woods and on the beaches near her family's Long Island home. Safe in the knowledge that the love and comfort of home and family were never far away, she loved to explore the outdoor world with her dogs, cats, and rabbits. As an adult, memories of her idyllic childhood days inspired Margaret Wise Brown to create picture books that have been cherished by generations of children.

Margaret Wise Brown was born in 1910 in New York City but moved to Long Island with

her family when she was three. As a teenager, Brown attended boarding schools in New York City; Lausanne, Switzerland; and Wellesley, Massachusetts. She graduated from Hollins College in 1932 with an English degree.

After college, Brown settled in New York City to seek a teaching career. She enrolled in the Cooperative School for Student Teachers run by the Bank Street School, a group of educators and scholars devoted to studying perception and learning in the very young. The Bank Street School was run by Lucy Sprague Mitchell, a woman who strongly believed that in order to educate young children one must understand and respect their unique view of the world, a view that cannot understand the past or the future, but only the "here and now."

After a few years as a student teacher, Brown decided that, although she still wanted to work with children, her true talent was not as a classroom instructor, but as a storyteller. Taking with her what she had learned about children's perception and learning at the Bank Street School, Brown gave up her student teaching in 1938 and embarked upon a new career as a writer. She accepted the job as children's book editor for publisher William R. Scott.

Before Margaret Wise Brown entered the world of children's books, picture books were considered throwaways aimed at an audience too young to truly learn, not true literature. Brown quickly changed existing attitudes by creating picture books that paired entertaining and educational stories for adults to read to their children with lively, colorful art that enhanced and expanded the story on a level that the youngest children could follow and enjoy. Brown paid special attention to her books' illustrations; she hoped that children would come back to and enjoy her books on their own, without the help of an adult narrator.

Brown's simple books viewed the world with a child's eye. They could be lighthearted, like *The Noisy Book,* which teaches children about the sounds around them with the help of a blind dog named Muffin, or they could be comforting, like *Goodnight Moon,* which offers a reassuring transition from daytime into the often frightening world of sleep. *The Runaway Bunny* seriously treats the common childhood fantasy of running away from home and allows the child to see through the experiences of the tiny rabbit that the comfort and security of home are what he or she truly wants and needs. In the world of Margaret Wise Brown's picture books, a child's thoughts, fears, and feelings are treated with respect and importance.

In all, Margaret Brown wrote, edited, or translated over one hundred books, many still treasured by children today. In 1947, she received The Caldecott Medal, one of the highest honors in her field, for *The Little Island.* In addition to her own name, Brown wrote under the pseudonyms of Golden MacDonald, Juniper Sage, and Timothy Hay. In an autobiographical sketch Brown once wrote that she wished to sign no name to her books, for she wanted nothing to come between the child and the story.

Margaret Wise Brown died in 1952. She never married and never had children of her own, yet she devoted her entire adult life to nurturing and educating the very young and providing laughter and comfort to countless children throughout the world. Brown once said that her goal in writing for children was "to make a child laugh or feel clear and happy headed . . . to lift him for a few moments from his own problems of shoe laces that won't tie and busy parents and mysterious clock time into the world of a bug or a bear or a bee or a boy living in the timeless world of a story." She achieved this goal by never forgetting the simple things that brought her joy in her own childhood—the woods and the beaches and the animals—and always remembering that the world of the child is a far different place than the world of an adult.

MY CRADLE DAYS

Loise Pinkerton Fritz

Take me back to my cradle days
    When I was very young;
Let Mother's hand caress my cheeks,
    Her lips peal forth a song.

A lullaby of go-to-sleep
    Till morning roosters crow
And sunbeams dance upon the quilt
    On the cradle marked and old.

Take me back to my cradle days,
    If time will but allow;
Let me feel the touch of Mother's hands
    Upon my tiny brow.

Let me see the smile upon her face
    As she rocks me to and fro;
Take me back to my cradle days
    And the Mother I love so.

CHILDHOOD DREAMING
Boston, Massachusetts
Dianne Dietrich Leis, Photographer

Maternal Song

Sudie Stuart Hager

How can I tell of a mother's worth?
By a song of the all-sustaining earth;
The earth that watches young
    plants rise
With arms outstretched to the
    distant skies;

The earth that gives them zeal to grow
But keeps their eager roots in tow;
That urges them to stand up proud,
Sustains them when their heads
    are bowed,

And strengthens them to face again
The thrusts of wind and hail and rain,
So they may bloom, bear fruit
    and seed,
To meet the hungering, tired
    world's need.

I sing of the kindly nurturing earth
To tell of a mother's priceless worth.

If I Could Give You a Perfect Day

Bertha Kleinman

If I could give you a perfect day,
　　O dearest mother of mine,
I know what the song on your lips would say
　　As your fingers twined in mine.
No thought of riches or worldly power
　　Would ever your dreaming be,
But the wish of your heart on that perfect day
　　Would be all in all for me.

When life shall give you a perfect day,
　　O dearest mother of mine,
The roses that carpet your twilight way
　　Must fall from these hands of mine.
Your wonderful love, like a shining ray,
　　Shall gladden the day's decline,
If I might be on that perfect day
　　The child of your heart's design!

© Archive Photos/Lambert

Five Stars for Mothers

There are stars for good spelling papers in school; there are stars for merit and valor in Government service; there are stars for quality on commercial products; there was a Star of Bethlehem to guide the Wise Men and the Shepherds to the little child who should lead a crusade for the brotherhood of man. Shall we not give the mothers a star for each of the roles which they play so faithfully?

Can you decide how many stars you would award to your mother, your favorite aunt, or the lady next door? Our horizons have been broadened. We must not narrow our margins to Maine, New York, Michigan, Texas, or Oregon. We hear, see, and feel beyond America. We must

begin to think, too, beyond America!

Shall we tuck our box of stars into our pockets and go forth to make our awards? As we broaden our minds and use our imaginations, we shall find that neither color nor country determines quality. We will understand how mothers and fathers everywhere are, in their way, helping to build a New Day for the world.

To whom should we award five stars? Let us examine the qualifications for human motherhood:

One star: She knows how to do with her own hands all the details of daily living, whether or not circumstances demand it of her. She thus teaches her children, and demonstrates to them

the dignity of all labor from the most menial task to the highest art.

Two star: She thinks in terms of values rather than costs, placing health in all its phases first among her family's goals. She teaches her children that sometimes one may be lonely when holding to high ideals. She understands how human nature changes as character develops, and she studies these changes as closely as she studies the price changes in her budget.

Three star: She herself grows in knowledge and wisdom that she may help her husband and her children toward the growth of fine individualities. She wants them all to be useful to themselves, their families, their community, and their country.

Four star: She knows that mother-love or father-love is a state of mind and heart which is existent in men and women whether they are married or not, whether they manage a home or not, and whether or not they have children. The four-star mother is not possessive. She knows that her child is not hers but God's. She knows that par-ents have the privilege of nurture, guidance, and love, but that the child's life is his own. She knows, too, that fathers share with mothers the protecting and guiding instinct toward the young, and she shows her appreciation for his sacrifices for the home.

Five star: She is a woman who believes in prayer and looks to her God for guidance. Of all the goodly heritage received from mothers, probably more than from any other quality, their faith in God, and their reliance upon prayer, have made more boys and girls keep fine, and more men and women return, after years of worldliness, to the sincerities of youth. When lonely and far from home, when friendless or in prison, men and women have found comfort in the memories of their mothers who read to them about God, taught them their prayers, and sang to them the hymns of some church.

It is a role more glorious than glamorous for those who would be five-star mothers.

Printed in *The Christian Science Monitor*, May 1, 1943.

Transient

Marie Hunter Dawson

I saw you sail your lavish craft,
A snow-white cloud on the sky's blue sea;
And suddenly you drifted down
In a petal shower from the apple tree.

You peeped from a clump of daffodils,
From arbutus and violets fresh with rain,
And adroitly posed in magic embrace
Your forsythia arms round our windowpane.

You dance in the willows whose bending plumes
Of yellow-green leaves sway the melodies.
I close my eyes and you sooth my cheek
With a breeze that has kissed the anemones.

You gleam in the raindrops, you laugh in the sun,
You sing as the birds call; and when you are gone,
All life is attuned to your buoyant ring,
And we live in the hope of another spring!

Readers' Forum

I received an *Ideals Mother's Day Magazine* this past Mother's Day, and I was so surprised to find that you are still around! I have *Ideals* magazines dated in the late 1950s and 1960s, and I used to always look at them as a child. I still look at those, and I really thought that *Ideals* was no longer in publication. Was I ever surprised! I love everything about the magazine and am so pleased to find the quality is still there. The photography, art, and poems are all inspiring to me . . . just like they always have been. I am so happy you are still around!

Carolyn Staples
Destin, Florida

Please renew my subscription of *Ideals Magazine* for two years. I have never received a magazine so magnificent . . . so meaningful. Receiving it is my personal hobby. I live and work on our dairy farm with my son and husband . . . and am so content and happy receiving your *Ideals Magazine*.

Mrs. James L. Fishpaw
Spring Grove, Pennsylvania

When I was a kid, I remember Edgar Guest's poems being in our daily newspaper. I saved every one I could get my hands on and saved them for a long time. But like a lot of things that get lost in moving around, the poems, too, got lost. I've always regretted that I didn't take better care of them, but now it warms my heart to read his poems again in *Ideals Magazine*. They always inspire a family feeling in me. . . . I love the magazine but that feature makes me really look forward to each issue.

Pauline Streeter
Springfield, Massachusetts

Editor's Note: The poetry of Edgar A. Guest is featured in every issue of Ideals *in* A Slice of Life. *In this issue, his poem can be found on pages 56-57.*

Editor's Note: Sharon Kraus of Nauvoo, Illinois, sent us this picture of her favorite gardeners as they prepare for their spring planting. Ideals *encourages all our readers to share their favorite pictures of grandchildren, children, and pets by sending them to the* Readers' Forum.

ideals
Celebrating Life's Most Treasured Moments